MY VIEWS

SERIES-1-FIFTY LIFE ORIENTED THOUGHTS

DR. A. JOHN PRADEEP EBENEZER

Copyright © Dr. A. John Pradeep Ebenezer
All Rights Reserved.

Dedicated to (Late) Master J. Allen Albert my beloved son who taught me the core values of life in short stint for 8 years in this world. I Know he is definitely in Heaven and he is rejoicing with God Almighty and i am hoping to meet him when my stint in this world is over. Catch you soon my son...

Contents

Preface

Most of the Thoughts portrayed in this book were the ones which I uploaded as status to ignite the young minds. Suddenly a Flash of Thoughts cross my minds and I just put it as my status. As i am meeting lot of young students daily, i am pretty sure that these thoughts has enlightened them and it paved a way for them to become succesfull in life. Glory be to God Almighty alone. Chapter-I list out the orginal thoughts that flashed my mind and i am very happy it has got shaped up in the form of this book. All other Chapters are the thoughts by famous personalities which brought me goosebumps and lifted me up when i am down.

CHAPTER ONE

Your Life- Rule it

1. Do you know why good is GOOD any guess !!!!! It's because BAD exist.

2. Every people living in this world are judged by their action (that is things what they do). My opinion is their actions are determined by their thoughts. **"Think about the thoughts that gives you thoughtful thinking"**.

3. The 2 BP's to keep your blood pressure under control. **"B"e "P"atient (your high BP becomes normal). "B"e. "P"ositive (your low BP becomes normal).**

4. Search for happiness begins by Going to a restaurant and ordering delicious dishes and finally envying the other tables menu. Going to a textile shop and seeing what others are wearing, Living with the loved ones but whatsapping with the remote stranger, Admiring others beauty. But...**My dear friends' happiness lies within us. Thank GOD for all the blessings and be a blessing to everyone.**

5. In life one can play any one of the two role **Defender, Underdog.** First let me tell u what they mean, Australia and Scotland is playing a cricket match then Australia can be called as defender because it is a number one team and it has won many matches and world cups. On

the other hand Scotland is an underdog because it is the team which is having a low profile in cricket. If you want to be as a defender you will have the following things , fame, money, stress and every day is a battle field. If you want to be as an underdog you will have Less fame, less money, without stress and nothing to lose in a day out. **"Be a defender in which area you are specialized and an underdog in rest of the things in life".**

6. Every one of us has a childhood dreams many of us will be striving very hard to make it into a reality. Some of us may have an ambition and will be working towards the goal to reach it. The BIG DRAMA is hidden here. The Question is how long our Quest should go in Chasing ones dream or an ambition should have a saturation point. We should try to be an UNSUNG HERO'S. No one remembers Kalpana chawla parents name or her mentor name the list is endless, the same applies for sachin, saina , sania. Heroes and Heroine's like sachins, sainas, sanias were made into a reality because of the UNSUNG HERO and UNSUNG HEROINES (i.e) their parents , mentors. **So draw a plimsoll line to your dreams and ambition and start nurturing your child if don't have one adopt one were you see the potential and become a UNSUNG HERO and UNSUNG HEROINE.**

7. Differences among people, friends, near and dear ones and nations can exist but that difference of opinion should not lead to problem or violence. **"EGO" is the the root cause of all evil. EGO is Evil is Giving Orders, Edging God Out, Edging Goodness Out. So my dear friends lead life with the affirmative response that is YES. EGO automatically flies out.**

8. In this world day by day we perform different gesture or we can call it as activities not all of them are recognized

or appreciated. Why?????????? "Whatever you do in this world do it with PASSION definitely you will reap the benefits".

9. The secret of success is Hard work???????Smart work?????Intelligence???????. **"One can follow the above mentioned things but still be unsuccessful the reason is we don't know the LIMITATIONS. If one comes to know about the limitations in the things what they do they can excel in life"**

10. **"The very existence of the fact GOD exist can be justified by the Presence of an invisible factor CONSCIENCE".** A person who is telling a lie knows he is committing it. A thief knows he is committing a mistake. The endless list goes on...My dear Friends GOD speaks from inside.

11. There is a saying which says "Look before you leap". There is a another saying "You cannot swim unless you are put on water". What is strange in these sayings? They are telling right the opposite. One saying tells think twice before you take any decision. Another saying tells us first get started with the things then try to swim in it. **"One important thing in achieving the impossible is taking the first step. Take it boldly and GOD will make u to swim in it."**

12. The statement "Give and it will be given to you" can be taken into discussion Don't give with the mentality that you will reap the benefits. **"Give as if there is no tomorrow", "Give and you have to give tomorrow, the days should roll on".** Nothing in this world gives pleasure as GIVING.

13. The world we live consist of many PLUS and MINUS. **"If we carefully look at this PL-US and MIN-US both includes US. We are responsible for this PLUS and**

MINUS. So try to change one MINUS into PLUS per day".

14. "Two person with same intelligence, hardwork, opportunity one succeeds another doesn't because of only one factor **PERSEVERANCE, PER+SEVERE+ANCE** which means **PER-One, SEVERE-vigorous, ANCE-action. Work continuously till the goal is reached.**

15. If your heart says that you are going to wipe away others tears and you are left wondering how to do it. **If you want to wipe away others TEARS just Take that T away and lend your EARS to them their TEARS will be changed into joy. Do you know Listening is an art?**

16. **"Don't hide yourself from PAIN you miss the GAIN".** God allows everyone one of us to go through trials and tribulation to get the best of us.

17. **Living in the world which opens up infinite opportunities to commit sin living a CHASTE life is the greatest achievement, live it till you breathe the last.**

18. **If you say I CAN you have taken a good decision. If you say I WILL achieve by the grace of God you are safe. After Achieving if you say I CAN ONLY it means you are SINKING.**

19. **"If you want to be inspirational to others always have a SMILE on your face, SMILE brings person MILE apart closer".**

20. **COURAGE is not doing things that should not or cannot be done. It is simply saying YES to YES and NO to NO.**

21. **WINNING is achieving what you can, not what you cannot. Many don't win because they don't know what they can. A WINNER should know what he or she can.**

22. "COMPARING is not knowing whether you are better than others, instead it is actually knowing how others perform the same task differently".

23. "Whether the World is winning you or You are winning the World". My dear friends there are many things in this world in which many of us are just a slave to it. God has given us Life to Win the World, Make it a better place and seek God's Glory".

24. "Helping others is Great, doing it when you are in Grief is Godly".

25. Your character lives longer than you, take care of your inner man/woman that is your reputation, whatever things you do, do it with a sense that God is watching you.

26. Basically there are three types of persons. A person who doesn't care about what is going around, A person who keeps on blabbering about the things that is going around, A person who knows what is going around and execute things. Judge yourself... You are in Which category.

27. To Climb a very high ALTITUDE in your Life ATTITUDE matters a lot ".

28. The need of the hour is doing right things in a right way at the right time. But what is very strange is we don't know what is right????? Right thinking can be poured on you if you acquire the following Asking for the will of God, Asking wisdom from God, Using Knowledge acquired from your teachers, Keeping your Soul clean.

29. Giving Hi....Fi's after victory boost your confidence but studying the Lo...Fi's after victory makes you stronger...

30. Happiness makes you lethargic , casual and saturated, whereas Sorrows makes you stronger, alert and

unsaturated.

31. Darkness is a place were light is given importance, were eyes are sharp, your mind is highly concentrating and you begin to think of others pain, so never mind when darkness is surrounding your life , you are actually tuned.

32. Flowing water sheds its impurities and adds up all the goodness into it while flowing but the stagnated water adds up All the impurities into it becoming still worse, Be a flowing water in life never stop when you encounter any obstacles add all the goodness replicate to others and be a blessing.

33. STOP worrying you will TOP the world.

34. TEARS sends a failure message to your EARS, which makes you weak, so stop CRYING start PRAYING.

35. Blending is the new mantra for success, Get into groove in whatever work you are put in like a coffee gets blended with milk I.e slowly and steadily.

36. How taking first step is important in reaching out for success, equally important is taking the last step because you never know how close you are to success.

37. Being like a Rock in life will make you to bear lot of sculpting hits to get moulded into shape, being as rubber band makes you fit into any groove with out getting any hits" Don't be stubborn, be flexy.

38. Travel the journey of life with PACIFYING PACE.

39. If you ASK God for a Blessing He will definitely show the TASK to get that Blessing.

40. Being a BLESSING to others is the greatest blessing on this planet Regards.

41. Do you know, KNOW has a NOW inside it , which is reminding us to KNOW the UNKNOWN NOW.

42. Live as if there is no tomorrow, be a Trendsetter not a Trend follower", the world needs you.

43. If OMG becomes GMO then you need not worry about the future" ,GMO- God is My Owner.

44. Every HEART knows the ART of aching others as well as the ART of consoling others it is up to your HEART to decide it.

45. In this world on any aspect of life many tend to do the easiest always , one such thing is PUSHING , it is easy pushing anything , that is pushing someone into a problem is easy, what is difficult in this world is PULLING , lending an helping hand to pull some one out of a Problem. Be a PULLER not a PUSHER. If you are a puller you bring others closer to you , if you are a pusher it is right the opposite.

46. PACESETTERS , they are people who sacrifice their self and make our life all at ease , that is we can sleep whole night peacefully because of the pacesetter army person, a dedicated doctor works for 24 hours setting us a pace of 8 hours of work per day, in marathon pacesetter decide the pace in which a winner should run , this endless list goes on spare a thought for pacesetter. Happy being a pacesetter than being a winner. Sometimes pacesetter also wins.

47. Know ones NEMESES then all your MISSES will fly away.

48. Following others FOOTPRINTS will make your FOOTPRINTS unprinted. Be an innovator.

49. Sharing normally happens with what we have that is if we are sad we share it when we are happy we share it, now think other way about the most difficult one share Happiness with others when you are sad. Share sadness with others when you are happy.

50. Being a down to earth person in life silently increases the respect what others have on you, more over that respect would come naturally not forcefully.

CHAPTER TWO

Warren Buffett-Thoughts-Goosebumps

This Chaper list out the Quotes by famous personality Mr. Warren Buffet which got me goosebumps.

<u>Warren Buffett</u>

1. The most important of the Warren Buffett quotes: "Rule No. 1 is never lose money. Rule No. 2 is never forget Rule No. 1.

2. Someone's sitting in the shade today because someone planted a tree a long time ago.

3. Price is what you pay, value is what you get.

4. Risk comes from not knowing what you are doing.

5. The most important investment you can make is in yourself.

6. I will tell you how to become rich. Close the doors. Be fearful when others are greedy. Be greedy when others are fearful.

7. Don't pass up something that's attractive today because you think you will find something better tomorrow.

8. Forecasts may tell you a great deal about the forecaster; they tell you nothing about the future.

9. We never want to count on the kindness of strangers in order to meet tomorrow's obligations. When forced

to choose, I will not trade even a night's sleep for the chance of extra profits.

10. No matter how great the talent or efforts, some things just take time. You can't produce a baby in one month by getting nine women pregnant

CHAPTER THREE

Bill Gates-Thoughts-Goosebumps

This Chaper list out the Quotes by famous personality Mr. Bill Gates which got me goosebumps.

1. Success is a lousy teacher. It seduces smart people into thinking they can't lose.
2. We all need people who will give us feedback. That's how we improve.
3. Patience is a key element of success.
4. The belief that the world is getting worse, that we can't solve extreme poverty and disease, isn't just mistaken. It's harmful.
5. Everyone needs a coach. It doesn't matter whether you're a basketball player, a tennis player, a gymnast, or a bridge player.
6. Don't compare yourself with anyone in this world ... if you do so, you are insulting yourself.
7. Your most unhappy customers are your greatest source of learning.
8. I can understand wanting to have millions of dollars, there's a certain freedom, meaningful freedom, that comes with that. But once you get much beyond that, I have to tell you, it's the same hamburger.

9. Television is not real life. In real life, people actually have to leave the coffee shop and go to jobs.
10. It's fine to celebrate success, but it is more important to heed the lessons of failure

CHAPTER FOUR

Dr. A. P. J. Abdul Kalam-Thoughts-Goosebumps

This Chaper list out the Quotes by famous personality Dr. A. P. J. Abdul Kalam which got me goosebumps.

1. If you want to shine like a sun, first burn like a sun.
2. Look at the sky. We are not alone. The whole universe is friendly to us and conspires only to give the best to those who dream and work.
3. Let us sacrifice our today so that our children can have a better tomorrow.
4. Writing is my love. If you love something, you find a lot of time. I write for two hours a day, usually starting at midnight; at times, I start at 11.
5. War is never a lasting solution for any problem.
6. You have to dream before your dreams can come true.
7. Teaching is a very noble profession that shapes the character, caliber, and future of an individual. If the people remember me as a good teacher, that will be the biggest honour for me.
8. Man needs his difficulties because they are necessary to enjoy success.
9. We should not give up and we should not allow the problem to defeat us.

10. If four things are followed - having a great aim, acquiring knowledge, hard work, and perseverance - then anything can be achieved.